D1264839

Smart Animals

ELEPHANTS

by Duncan Searl

Consultant: Michael McClure
Elephant Manager
The Maryland Zoo in Baltimore

BEARPORT
PUBLISHING COMPANY, INC.

New York, New York

Credits

Cover (background), Alex Bramwell/istockphoto; Cover (center), Mark Wilson/
istockphoto; Title Page, Mark Wilson/istockphoto; 4, Courtesy of Bali Adventure Tours
Elephant Conservation Foundation; 5, Courtesy of The Phoenix Zoo; 6, Images of Africa
Photobank/Alamy; 7, James J. Stachecki/Animals Animals, Earth Scenes; 8, Ian
Redmond; 9(t), Peter Steiner/Alamy; 9(b), David Boag/Alamy; 10, © age fotostock/
SuperStock; 11(t), Dave Herring; 11(b), Frans Lanting/Minden Pictures; 12, © Keith
Scholey/naturepl.com; 13, Photolibrary.com; 14, The Granger Collection; 15, Mickey
Gibson/Animals Animals, Earth Scenes; 16, © Tony Heald/naturepl.com; 17, © Simon
King/naturepl.com; 18, Frans Lanting/Minden Pictures; 19(t), Peter Lillie OSF;
19(b), Gerry Ellis/Minden Pictures; 20, John Cancalosi/Peter Arnold, Inc.; 21, Infocus
Photos, Alamy; 22, The Granger Collection; 23, Frans Lanting/Minden Pictures; 24, Dave
Herring; 25, © NHPA/Jonathan Angela Scott; 26, Steve Bloom Images/Alamy; 28(l), Allen
Photography/Animals Animals, Earth Scenes; 28(r), © GHANI, KHALID/Animals
Animals, Earth Scenes; 29 (l), Neil Budzinski, courtesy of Mulatta Records (www.mulatta.
org); 29 (r), Jerry Alexander, courtesy of Mulatta Records (www.mulatta.org).

Design and production by Dawn Beard Creative and Octavo Design and Production, Inc.

Library of Congress Cataloging-in-Publication Data

Searl, Duncan.
  Elephants / by Duncan Searl.
     p. cm.—(Smart animals!)
  Includes bibliographical references and index.
  ISBN 1-59716-162-4 (library binding)—ISBN 1-59716-188-8 (pbk.)
  1. Elephants—Juvenile literature. 2. Animal intelligence—Juvenile literature. I. Title.
II. Series.

  QL737.P98S43 2006
  599.67—dc22
                        2005026828

For more information, write to Bearport Publishing Company, Inc., 101 Fifth Avenue,
Suite 6R, New York, New York 10003. Printed in the United States of America.

1 2 3 4 5 6 7 8 9 10

Contents

Elephant Art 4

Quick Thinking 6

Using Tools 8

A Trunk Full of Surprises 10

Passing on Information 12

Working Elephants 14

Emotional Intelligence 16

Elephant Talk 18

Elephant Reunions 20

Solving Problems 22

Saving Wild Elephants 24

Always Learning, Always Teaching 26

Just the Facts 28

More Smart Elephants 29

Glossary 30

Bibliography 31

Read More 31

Learn More Online 31

Index 32

About the Author 32

Elephant Art

Ramona (ruh-MOH-nuh) picks up her brush. She dips it in some yellow paint. Then she goes to work. After a few strokes, Ramona switches to red paint, then green. Like other artists, she looks carefully at her work. Ramona is not like most painters, though. She's an elephant in an animal **safari park**.

▲ **The money from Ramona's paintings is used to help save elephants in the wild.**

Why do the park rangers give Ramona paint and brushes? Elephants don't like standing around doing nothing. They're too smart for that. Painting gives Ramona something interesting to do.

Ramona gets some peanuts for finishing each painting. However, she isn't just working for peanuts. Some of her paintings sell for $2,000!

◀ **Ruby was a well-known elephant artist at the Phoenix Zoo. She was known for matching the colors in her paintings to the colors of people's clothes.**

Dozens of elephants in zoos and parks enjoy painting pictures.

Quick Thinking

Elephants began painting only recently. However, people have known for a long time that elephants are smart.

In ancient Rome, people liked to watch wild animals fight. Sometimes they made an elephant fight a rhino. It was a cruel thing to do.

▲ **This wild elephant attacks a Cape buffalo in Africa.**

Elephants tend to be peaceful. When threatened, however, they are fierce fighters.

Once, during a fight, an elephant saw a long metal rod on the ground. Right away, he picked it up with his **trunk**. Then he stuck it in the rhino's eyes. Unable to see, the rhino lost the fight.

No one had taught the elephant how to use the rod as a **weapon**. He was smart enough to figure it out by himself.

▲ **In the wild, elephants usually get along with other animals. These elephants are sharing a water hole with zebras and a giraffe.**

Using Tools

Ramona and the elephant in ancient Rome both used **tools**—a paintbrush and a metal rod. Using tools is a sure sign of **intelligence**.

What other tools do elephants use? Elephants often use sticks to scratch their backs. Sometimes they throw old tires up into trees to weigh down the branches. Then they can reach the leaves and fruit. Elephants have even used logs to break down stone walls.

▲ **An elephant using a branch to scratch his ear**

After humans and apes, elephants are the most likely animals to use tools.

In Africa, some elephants figured out how to open a village water **faucet**. To stop the elephants, the villagers bolted the faucet shut. The animals then used rocks to break the nuts and bolts on the faucet.

This elephant cools off by using a hose. ▶

▲ **Elephants may bend trees to scratch themselves.**

A Trunk Full of Surprises

To hold tools, people use their hands. Elephants, however, use their trunks.

Elephants mainly use their trunks to eat and drink. They pick up food with their trunks. They also suck in water through their trunks and then spray it into their mouths.

◀ **With its trunk, an elephant can reach food 19 feet (6 m) off the ground.**

The trunk is a sensitive nose. The **nostrils** on the tip of a trunk can smell water 12 miles (19 km) away!

There are two main kinds of elephants—Asian and African. Asian elephants have one "finger" on the tip of their trunks. African elephants have two "fingers." These fingers are delicate enough to pick up a blade of grass or a tiny peanut. At the same time, the trunk is powerful enough to grab a lion and crush it to death.

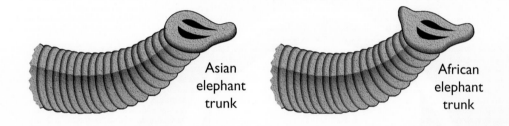

Asian elephant trunk

African elephant trunk

▲ **When an elephant swims underwater, it uses its trunk as a snorkel.**

Passing on Information

Teaching is another sign of intelligence. When elephants learn something, they pass on the information. For example, older elephants show their young, or **calves**, where to dig for water in the dry season.

All **mammals**, such as elephants, need salt to live. Sometimes, however, elephants don't get enough salt through the plants they eat. So they have to lick it directly from the ground.

▲ **Elephant digging for salt**

It's not always easy to find salt, though. So older elephants show their calves the places to find it, such as in caves. In this way, age-old knowledge is passed down from one **generation** to the next.

▲ **Elephants learn from other elephants where to dig in caves for salt. These African elephants walk as far as 492 feet (150 m) in pitch-black darkness to find salt.**

Being able to share knowledge helps an elephant **herd** survive.

Working Elephants

Since elephants are good learners, people put them to work. Long ago, elephants were trained for war. They carried soldiers and weapons into battle, like living tanks.

▲ **The sight of a war elephant was enough to frighten many enemies.**

In the days before tractors and bulldozers, elephants did much of the heavy work in India and Southeast Asia. They moved huge logs and heavy stones. They plowed fields for crops. Elephants helped build roads and railroads, too. Today, they still do some of this work in Southeast Asia.

▲ **Elephants will only work for handlers whom they trust.**

In India, an elephant trainer or handler is called a mahout (muh-HOWT).

Emotional Intelligence

The actions of elephants show they are smart. Yet these huge animals also show their intelligence through their emotions, or feelings.

For example, elephants **grieve**. When a baby elephant dies, its mother stands by its side for days. The mother's head and ears hang down sadly. The corners of her mouth turn down. At this sorrowful time, the mother's movements are slow and quiet.

▲ **This elephant guards the body of a dead herd member.**

Young elephants sometimes see their mothers killed by **poachers**. These orphans are filled with grief. In the weeks that follow, they often wake up at night screaming, as if they are having a nightmare.

Sometimes elephants come across elephant skeletons. They may stop in silence and touch the bones or **tusks** with their trunks. They may even carry the bones with them for a while.

Elephant Talk

Communication is another way to measure animal intelligence. Elephants use about 30 different sounds to communicate with one another.

Some elephant sounds travel for six miles (10 km) or more. They help herd members stay in touch over long distances. Some elephant calls have a very **low frequency**. These sounds are so low that humans can't hear them.

▲ **Females and young males live in elephant herds. An elephant herd is led by a matriarch, the oldest and wisest female.**

Elephants also use **body language** to communicate. For example, the main elephant in a herd might flap her ears hard against her body. The flapping means "Time to go. Follow me." When the ears are straight back, it means "Watch out!"

▲ **Elephant flapping ears**

Elephants make sounds in their throats. The sounds get louder as they vibrate through the trunk.

Elephant Reunions

Elephant **reunions** show how the animals communicate excitement or joy. Elephants normally greet one another with a rumbling sound. The loudness of the rumble depends on how long they've been separated. Elephants rumble louder when they meet old friends and family members.

▲ Elephants may say "hello" by wrapping their trunks around each other.

When elephants have been separated from a friend for a long time, their reunion is really loud! They rush together wildly and spin around. Their ears flap with excitement. Ear-splitting trumpeting sounds fill the air.

▲ **Young elephants greeting**

Elephants make a purring sound when they are pleased to meet another elephant. They make loud growls and roars when feeling pain.

Solving Problems

Sometimes elephants find creative solutions to problems. A story from Myanmar (MEEYAN-mar), a country in Southeast Asia, shows how.

Elephants in one village loved to eat bananas. So the villagers hung bells around the animals' necks. The bells let the people hear the elephants if they tried to steal bananas from their trees.

▲ This painting of an Asian nobleman riding an elephant is about 400 years old. Yet people and elephants have lived together in Asia for thousands of years.

The elephants, however, would not be so easily outsmarted. They went to the river and filled the bells with mud. When the mud dried, the bells didn't ring. The elephants could now steal all the bananas they wanted.

Depending on an elephant's size, the animal can eat between 200 and 350 pounds (91–159 kg) of food a day.

Saving Wild Elephants

Although elephants are smart, they need people's help to survive. As farms and cities expand, there is less room for elephants. The **habitats** of these huge animals are shrinking. To protect elephants, nations have to set aside parks and **reserves** for them.

Elephants in the Wild

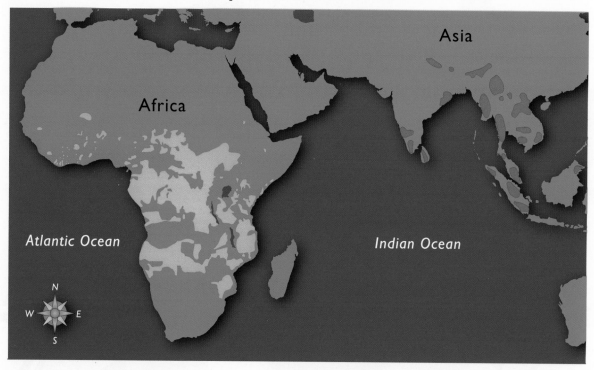

Range of African elephant

Range of Asian elephant

▲ **Only 35,000–50,000 Asian elephants survive in the wild. About 600,000 elephants live in Africa.**

Illegal hunting, or poaching, is another problem. Hunters kill elephants for their tusks. The tusks are made of **ivory**, which is very valuable. For elephants to survive, poaching must stop.

Tusks are actually overgrown teeth. They are used as tools for digging and as weapons during fighting.

▲ **Thousands of African elephants have been killed for their tusks.**

Always Learning, Always Teaching

In recent years, people have built electric fences to keep elephants off their land. In some places, however, the elephants were too smart. The giant animals learned how to drop logs on the fence wires. They also used the tips of their tusks to break the wires. Then the elephants taught these skills to their calves.

As in the past, these elephants showed that they're smart enough to use tools. In addition, they can communicate and pass along what they learn. These brainy beasts not only have giant brains, they know how to use them.

Elephants have the biggest brain of any land mammal. However, a few animals, such as chimps and orangutans, are considered by most scientists to be even smarter than elephants.

Just the Facts

	African Elephant	**Asian Elephant**

Weight	8,000–15,000 pounds (3,629–6,804 kg)	6,000–11,000 pounds (2,722–4,990 kg)
Height (at shoulder)	10–13 feet (3–4 m)	6–10 feet (2–3 m)
Highest Point on Body	on shoulder	top of head
Skin	wrinkly	smooth
Ear Size	large	small
Tusks	males and females have tusks	only males may have tusks
Tip of Trunk	has two "fingers"	has one "finger"
Food	mainly leaves	mainly grass
Life Span	about 65 years	about 65 years
Habitat	grasslands and forests in Africa	grasslands, rain forests, and swamps in Asia

More Smart Elephants

In India, an elephant was chained up beside a river. Heavy rains began, and the elephant sank deeper and deeper into the mud. Frightened, he broke off branches from a nearby tree and stood on them. That way, he stayed safe until his handler returned.

The Thai Elephant Orchestra makes amazing music. The musicians—all of them are elephants—play giant-sized drums, gongs, xylophones, and harmonicas. There's even an elephant keyboard.

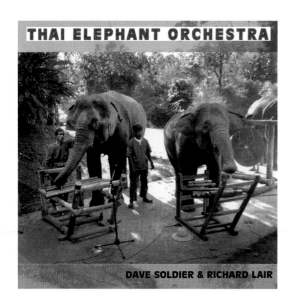

Glossary

body language (BOD-ee LANG-gwij) body movements used to share information

calves (KAVZ) young elephants

communication (kuh-*myoo*-nuh-KAY-shuhn) the passing along of information

faucet (FAW-sit) a device that lets one turn the flow of water on and off

generation (*jen*-uh-RAY-shuhn) a group of people or animals that were born around the same time

grieve (GREEV) feel very sad

habitats (HAB-uh-*tats*) places in nature where animals are usually found

herd (HURD) a large group of animals that feed and travel together

intelligence (in-TEL-uh-juhns) the ability to understand, solve problems, and learn

ivory (EYE-vur-ee) a hard white material that forms elephant tusks

low frequency (LOH FREE-kwuhn-see) very low sounds

mammals (MAM-uhlz) animals that are warm-blooded, nurse their young with milk, and have hair or fur on their skin

nostrils (NOSS-truhlz) openings in the nose that are used for breathing and smelling

poachers (POHCH-urz) people who hunt illegally

reserves (ri-ZURVZ) places where animals are protected so that they can safely live

reunions (ree-YOON-yuhnz) meetings between animals or people who have not been together for a long time

safari park (suh-FAH-ree PARK) a zoo or reserve where animals roam freely

tools (TOOLZ) objects that are used to help do a job

trunk (TRUHNGK) the long nose of an elephant

tusks (TUHSKS) long, pointed teeth, such as those on an elephant or walrus, that are often used for fighting or digging

weapon (WEP-uhn) something that is used to hurt someone

Bibliography

Alexander, Shana. *The Astonishing Elephant.* New York: Random House (2000).

Douglas-Hamilton, Iain, and Oria Douglas-Hamilton. *Among the Elephants.* New York: Viking Press (1975).

Payne, Katy. *Silent Thunder: In the Presence of Elephants.* New York: Simon & Schuster (1998).

Shoshani, Dr. Jeheskel, ed. *Elephants: Majestic Creatures of the Wild.* New York: Rodale Press (1992).

Read More

George, Dick. *Ruby: The Painting Pachyderm of the Phoenix Zoo.* New York: Delacorte Press (1995).

Redmond, Ian. *Elephants.* Lovingston, VA: Bookwrights Press (1990).

Schmidt, Jeremy. *In the Village of the Elephants.* New York: Walker & Company (1994).

Learn More Online

Visit these Web sites to learn more about elephants:

www.sandiegozoo.org/animalbytes/t-elephant.html

www.worldwildlife.org/elephants

Index

Africa 6, 9, 24

African elephant 11, 13, 24–25, 28

ancient Rome 6, 8

Asia 22, 24

Asian elephant 11, 24, 28

body language 19

calves 12–13, 26

caves 13

communication 18–19, 20–21, 27

emotional intelligence 16–17

grieving 16–17

habitats 24, 28

India 15, 29

ivory 25

mahout 15

painting 4–5, 6, 8

poachers 17, 25

problem-solving 22–23

Ramona 4–5, 8

reunions 20–21

Ruby 5

salt 12–13

Southeast Asia 15, 22

teaching 12–13, 26–27

Thai Elephant Orchestra 29

tool use 8–9, 10, 25, 27

trunk 7, 10–11, 17, 19, 20, 28

tusks 17, 25, 26, 28

war elephants 14

working elephants 14–15

About the Author

Duncan Searl is a writer and editor who lives in New York. He is the author of many books for young readers.